From
Personal Ads
to Cloning Labs

From
Personal Ads
to Cloning Labs

More Science Cartoons from
Sidney Harris

W. H. Freeman and Company
New York

Library of Congress Cataloging-in-Publication Data

Harris, Sidney.
  From Personal Ads to Cloning Labs; More Cartoons from Sidney Harris.
    p. cm.
  ISBN 0-7167-2351-4
  1. Science – Caricatures and cartoons. 2. American wit and humor,
Pictorial. I. Title.
NC1429.H33315A4 1992   92-1606
                                                          CIP

All the contents of this book have been previously published and
copyrighted by the following periodicals, *Air & Space, American Scientist,*
Chronical of Higher Education, Clinical Chemistry News, Discover,
Fantasy and Science Fiction, Hippocrates, Johns Hopkins Magazine, Physics
Today, Science, Science '80, The New Yorker, Today's Chemist and a few
extinct publications. Special thanks to Ed Ferman for giving Dr. Quark
a somewhat steady job.

© 1993 by Sidney Harris

Printed in the United States of America

1 2 3 4 5 6 7 8 9 0 RRD 9 9 8 7 6 5 4 3 2

From
Personal Ads
to Cloning Labs

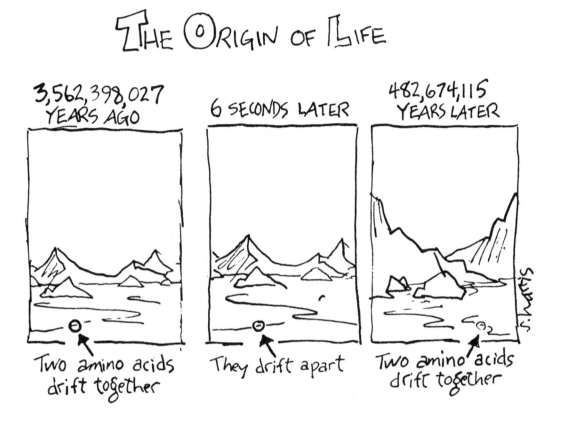

"We're picking up the birth of a star, and the death of a star.
The only problem is, it seems to be the same star."

"Our portions come in three sizes: Bit, Byte and Megabyte."

"I'll say this for the invertebrates—they probably never get backaches."

"I'll have them coming and going—this is the new Bunsen Fire Extinguisher."

"According to the voice-stress analyzer, he's *not* going to lower taxes."

"Frankly, I have a lot of trouble relating to all this symbolism."

"You must clear your mind. You must concentrate. You must focus. Then you will find it is an easy matter to hit a low, outside fast ball."

"It's not encroaching civilization that's threatening our way of life—it's the encroaching hordes of primate-life researchers who are doing it."

HUMAN SILICON CHIP:
CAPABLE OF 6 COMPUTATIONS PER HOUR

"True, my last several experiments fizzled, and a year's work has gone down the drain, but I'm not discouraged. My video game 'Antigens and Antibodies' is selling like hotcakes."

Mozart writing the digital version of his symphony No. 38 in D major.

"From the variety of objects found here—cooking utensils, furniture, tools, games—and the multi-levels on which they are found, I'd say we have come across man's earliest shopping mall."

"It's just not working. *He's* teaching *me* primate speech."

"I think you've crossed that thin line between transmuting and cooking."

"Maybe it *is* a closed universe."

CHARLES DARWIN SLIDING INTO THIRD WITH HIS REALIZATION THAT THE FITTEST SURVIVE

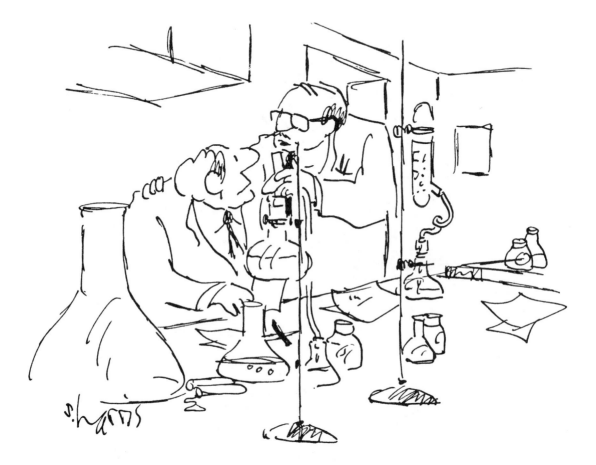

"I think you've done it. All we need now is a trademark and a theme song."

ALEXANDER GRAHAM BELL, MAKING THE FIRST CALL FROM NEW YORK TO CHICAGO GETS A WRONG NUMBER

BIZARRE SEQUENCE OF COMPUTER-GENERATED RANDOM NUMBERS

"Have you come across any of the rare earths—praseodymium, gadolinium, dysprosium—stuff like that?"

"I'm sorry, Professor Minskov, but that article on Minskov's Theory . . . they want someone else to write it."

"I see they predict melting of the polar ice cap. Wonder how that will affect us."

"I love to hear the pitter-patter-patter-patter-patter-patter-patter-patter-patter-patter-patter-patter-patter-patter-patter-patter-patter-patter-patter of his tiny feet."

"It *didn't* work? Did you stir it?"

"No, this isn't low temperature physics. He's just too cheap to turn on the heat."

"Well, well—this should create a nice little wave of panic and hysteria."

SOFT DRINK MADE OF ELEMENTARY PARTICLES (MESONS) WITH ANOMALOUSLY LONG LIFE

"You're *supposed* to have a ringing in your ears. That's what echo-location is all about."

"We'll have to get rid of all our furniture. They just discovered perspective."

"It figures. If there's artificial intelligence, there's bound to be some artificial stupidity."

"I can help you with tiny, little steps. As for breakthroughs, you're on your own."

"Don't add potassium nitrate to *anything* this year."

"What an ego! One day it's Newton's Laws of Dynamics, then it's
Newton's Theory of Gravitation, and Newton's Law of
Hydronamic Resistance, and Newton's This and Newton's That."

"My specialty is the small woodland mammal—its physiology, its genetics, its symbiotic relationships and its place in children's literature."

"Now that it can communicate with other computers, it says it doesn't want to communicate with us."

"Another advantage of genetic engineering: viruses you can *see*!"

"The environment people know we're an endangered species, the hunters know we're an endangered species . . . if only the lions knew we're an endangered species."

"While we're working on the secret of life, Dr. Helmholz, there, is trying to unravel its meaning."

"Ignore him. He's a hypochondriac."

"What we especially like about these theoretical types is that they don't tie up thousands of dollars worth of equipment."

"You can't come into the clean room looking like that!"

"It's an excellent proof, but it lacks warmth and feeling."

"Just what we need—mass transit."

"They didn't tell *me* what to do with it. I thought they told *you* what to do with it."

"I gave it the traveling salesman problem. It said he should give up
sales and go into banking."

"It's a new, high-protein substitute for soybean paste. It's made of steak."

"It's our new assembly line. When the person at the end of the line has an idea, he puts it on the conveyor belt, and as it passes each of us, we mull it over and try to add to it."

HARMFUL FOOD ADDITIVES

COAL

ROPE

TWO OF CLUBS

THE ED WITTEN STRING-THEORY QUARTET

"I'm strictly a squid and seaweed eater. Whenever I have plankton, I'm hungry an hour later."

It's simple. If my breakthrough becomes the property of the company, I won't tell you what it is."

"That's science. We send probes to Mars—Mars sends probes to Earth."

"I think . . . yes . . . his name is here on the door: A. Van Leeuwenhoek."

"You simply associate each number with a word, such as 'Table' and 3,476,029."

"Should we walk upright? Should we continue to live in trees? Should we try to make things? Decisions, decisions!"

"You never go to your counting-house any more."

"The Chloride Co. wants to merge with us. They think we can make salt together."

"It's beginning to show *some* human characteristics—faulty reasoning, forgetfulness and repetition."

"I must say it isn't easy adjusting to a 24-second day."

"This is going to set oceanography back 50 years."

"This universe will either continue expanding at its present rate, expand at a slower rate, or it will begin to contract. None of this, however, can account for the fact that it sometimes takes four days to get a letter from Chicago."

"That, in itself, is a breakthrough."

"As an anthropologist, I've been to tropic jungles and frozen tundras. I've seen primitive cultures and sophisticated societies. But this is the only place where I've have been unable to figure out what's going on."

THE FIRST PERSON WHO CLEARED HIS THROAT

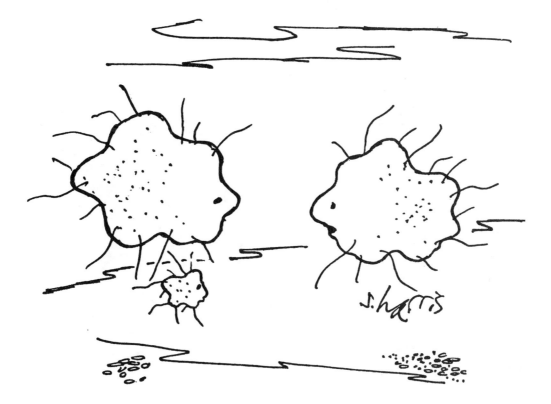

"He looks just like you. But he looks just like me, too."

"You see fewer and fewer of them these days. They're probably becoming extinct."

"Your problem is in the gene which makes antibodies, but since the Biophase Corp. now has a patent on that gene, I can't do anything for you."

CHAOS: THE CARTOON

S. Harris

"If he presses the first lever, some food comes out. If he presses the second lever, some candy comes out. If he presses the third lever a female mouse comes out. After a week of this, he's looking for another lever."

"He has a pre-Copernican attitude about himself—believes he's the center of the universe."

"On some pictures, my right brain says they're good art, but my left brain says they're bad investments. On others, my right brain says they're bad art, but my left brain says they're good investments."

"But if you need someone for the *intangibles* . . ."

"He said 'Rocco no speak more word not give you tell secret have,' and I think he means he can't express anything very subtle with the limited vocabulary we gave him."

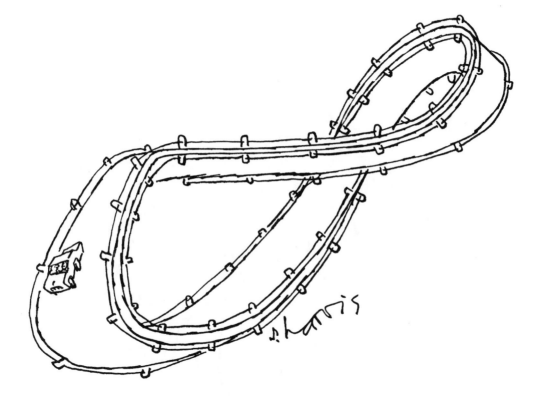

"Mobius? Who's Mobius?"

"Frankly, *I* even find it hard to believe some of the things I've been coming up with."

"I've heard of continental drift, but this is ridiculous."

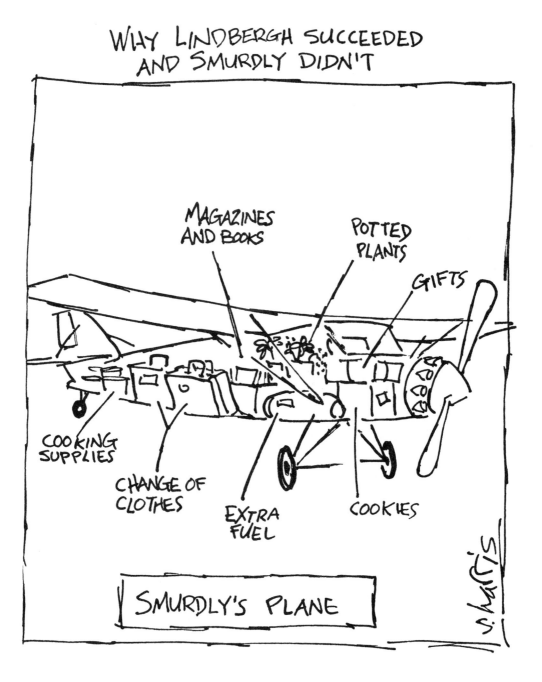

"Geology to the left of us. Geology to the right of us. Wherever we look, geology. And we can get in on the ground floor."

"I can remember when everyone was skeptical about the
greenhouse effect."

"As I understand it, our reactions were so remarkable, *we're* getting the Nobel prize."

Leonardo da Vinci awakes in the middle of the night to review his plans for a flying machine, and, half asleep, is unable to read his own reverse handwriting.

S. Harris

"I'll tell you why we're becoming extinct. Because we're solitary creatures, even during the *mating* season—that's why we're becoming extinct."

"I've been tagged by a wildlife commission, some environment people, an agriculture research team, some zoologists, a government group . . ."

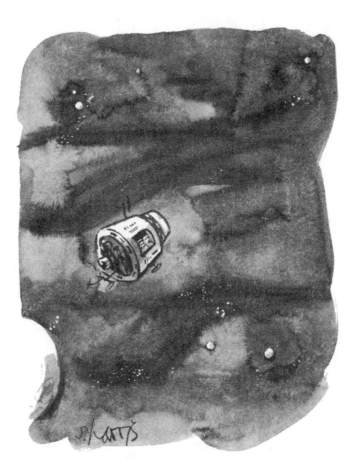

"It's always that way—whenever you want to get someplace fast, it seems as if the universe is rapidly expanding."

"I like the Pasteurs, but my goodness—boiled tomato juice, boiled fish with boiled lettuce, boiled bread and boiled butter, boiled salad . . ."

THE RAIN FOREST: BIG CITY FOR ANIMALS

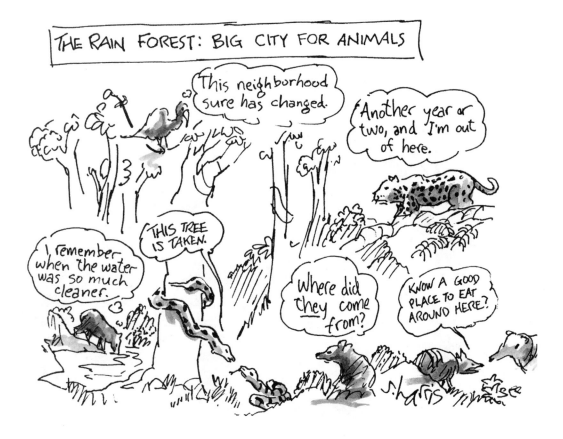

"It's a good thing I built this place when I did. The new zoning law prevents any house from going over 75,000 calories."

"Is that it? Is that the Grand Unified Theory?"

"Don't forget—keep the potassium chloride in a
separate container."

"Remember—a breakthrough is not a breakthrough unless you coin a term for it."

"If we didn't do so well in the easy box, they wouldn't have given us this complicated box."

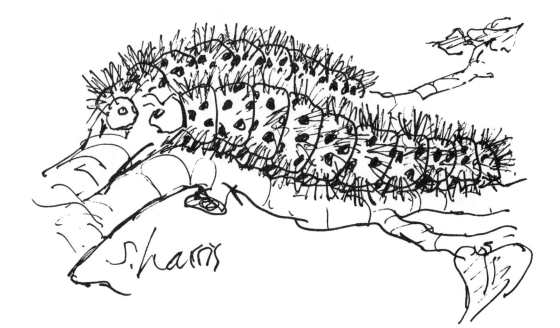

"Well, you could just forget about changing into a grasshopper, and that's that."

"Well, this should give us some valuable insight into the origin of the universe."

Testimonials

"Thank you for writing *You Live Forever*. It was wonderful, and I have shared it several times."

Clara George, Missouri

"Never in my wildest dreams would I ever expect someone I know would have an experience like you … this book…was wonderful. Thank you."

Twila & Bob Stapel, Kansas

"This book was wonderful and beautiful, I find it easy to believe. My mother saw an angel when she died."

Iris Wylie, Missouri

"I read your book and found it beautiful. Can I send it to other people?"

Karen Thompson, Arizona

"Erma and I really enjoyed your book. We thought it was wonderful. We are grateful you came back to share it with us."

Your brother, John Thompson, Arizona

"We so enjoyed your book. I truly believe you saw what you saw … you were blessed."

Omega Cole, Illinois

" That was beautiful and has increased my belief. Thanks for sharing."

Nadeane Wood, Kansas

"I really enjoyed your book. It gave me peace of mind. I think God is telling us something."

Beth Uber, Illinois

1

"Thanks for sharing your story. I believe it. There is no doubt that God has great things waiting for us. Keep writing."

George Ogan, Kansas

"Your book is an inspiration, Gladys. I read your account of our meeting at the Topeka and Shawnee County Public Library, and I can vouch for the fact it's accurate. God put us together to get this book to everyone who needs your reassuring message that God is Love and that Angels watch over us."

Esther Luttrell, Kansas

In Memory of My Husband
Warren R. Hargis

You Live Forever, You Live Forever... / Gladys Hargis

You Live Forever
You Live Forever
You Live Forever

Revised Edition

"I am only the messenger"
Gladys Hargis

Gladys Hargis

5

You Live Forever, You Live Forever... / Gladys Hargis

You Live Forever, You Live Forever, You Live Forever

Copyright © 2016 by Gladys L. Hargis

Revised edition

Previously published as *You Life Forever,* West Bow Press. *(*2010)

ISBN-13 : 978-15533236531
ISBN -10 : 1533236534

Printed in the USA

Dedicated to my childhood friend

Beth Jeffries Uber

You Live Forever, You Live Forever... / Gladys Hargis

PROLOGUE

This is my true story about having a near death experience in August 2006. I can only tell you what I saw, yet there are no words to describe it all. It was beautiful and beyond description. It has changed my life forever, and I witness about it every chance I get.

I wrote this book because I want to tell everyone what I saw beyond this world. I know for a fact it was real, because usually when you dream, you wake up and cannot remember all of the details, only sketches. These experiences, however, are imprinted in my memory, and will be there for my lifetime

There are Angels present long before your soul leaves your body. When your body is sinking, they will make their presence known.

This book is intended to ease the pain and separation of family and friends that we all have to endure..

God and his Angels will be with you always, so have no fear.

I hope you enjoy reading *You Live Forever* as much as I have enjoyed writing it.

Gladys L. Hargis
Topeka, Kansas

You Live Forever, You Live Forever... / Gladys Hargis

ACKNOWLEDGMENTS

I want to thank my niece Ruth Ann Maus, who had medical knowledge, and encouraged the doctors at Stormont Vail Hospital in Topeka Kansas to try everything they could to save my life, because no one knew what was wrong with me. I was told later that, at times they almost gave up hope.

I want to thank the Topeka Fire Department who arrived first and tried to stabilize me.

I thank the American Medical Response team who took over and worked to keep me breathing.

My thanks to Dr. Kingfisher and his assistants in the emergency room, who brought me back to life not just once but twice. I was put on life support until they could determine the cause of my condition. When I once asked if I was going to live, I heard someone in the room shout, "Yes, you are", which was encouraging.

A special thanks to Dr. Arfaei, Dr. Malik, Dr. Graham, Dr. Gandhi, Dr. Patel, Dr. Leeds, Dr. Ta, and hospital consultant, Dr. McKee.

Thank you, Dr. Rankin, and all of the nurses in the ICU unit who watched over me every minute of the eight days I was in intensive care.

I especially thank Rose Marie Steenhoven, Rene, and Jeanette, nurses on Stormont Veil's sixth floor, who took care of me on my long road back to recovery.

I thank the Angels who watched over me and gave me the courage to want to live. The other world is so peaceful I can hardly wait to return, but I have a job to do.

A special thanks to my sister Joy Law, who came to my bedside and kept me lucid,, asking questions about what I saw in Heaven, and whether or not Angels have wings.

In truth, I was so excited about my incredible journey that I had to tell someone who would listen to my stories.

Joy said later that I had awakened once singing *Bringing in the Sheaves.* The staff in ICU, and my sister, said I sang every verse. I didn't think I even knew every verse.

I, indeed, must have seen something wonderful when I had a close brush with death. Dr. Arfaei, my lung doctor, believed my story and even acknowledged to others that he was certain I actually had those experiences. .

I thank Heidi Kuglin for her help and support.

On Valentine's Day, 2010, my Presbyterian minister, Pastor Bob Hattle, used part of this book in his sermon. I thank him for that.

And, finally, a special thanks to my husband, Warren, who was with me continually throughout this ordeal. He was, as I was, in awe of what I had seen on my journey into the other world. He, too, was given a great gift when he witnessed an Angel watching over me in my hospital room. It made a believer out of him, and he thanked God every day for the honor.

I hope this book brings you peace and the acknowledgement that *love* conquers all, and that GOD is great.

TABLE OF CONTENTS

PART I

You Live Forever, You Live Forever... / Gladys Hargis

1

The Doorway to Heaven

One Friday afternoon, as we sat on the porch enjoying an Indian summer, my husband Warren and I were talking about a couple who had died within days of each other. Warren and I were married for more than fifty-seven years , and we agreed that it would be a wonderful gift to go to Heaven as our friends had gone; at nearly the same time.

Warren laughingly said, "Why don't you go first. I'll see that you get the songs you want at your funeral and give you a great send off."

"If you go first," I answered, "I'll let everyone watch your old Gene Autry movies while listening to country western songs."

We had no idea what the next two days would bring.

The next day, I went to my water-walking class at the local YMCA. Afterward, I began to have trouble walking. Getting to my car took a lot of effort. When I got home, I elevated my feet and legs, and rested. Later the next day, my legs and arms began to swell.

Because it was a Saturday, I decided to wait until Monday morning to see the doctor, but by 7:30 that evening I was filling up with liquid at an alarming rate. I asked Warren to call an ambulance, adding, "Please tell them not to use their lights and sirens. I don't want to entertain the neighborhood." Of course, I forgot the fire department would come with their big red truck, lights flashing, sirens blaring, attracting neighbors from blocks away.

Not wanting me to realize how worried he was, Warren joked, "We should have fixed some popcorn to sell. We could have made some money."

I was able to walk to the gurney and lie down. I remember looking up at Warren and my niece Ruth Ann. She lived next door and had come over when the firemen arrived. After that, everything turned black. I arrived at the Stormont Vail Hospital emergency room in a coma, nearly DOA.

When I was resuscitated in the emergency room I realized that my body was shutting down. I could, literally, feel my life draining away. I heard my niece and my husband say that my feet were black and that my skin was pale gray. I could hear the doctors trying to decide what was wrong with me.

I knew I was not going to live, but I was not afraid. I told whoever was listening to tell my husband that I loved him, and to get hold of my son. And then I went into a coma. That's when I visited a wonderful place.

Actually, 1 was given a glimpse of Heaven many times during the next eight days.

2

I've Got a Secret

First, I was in a hallway, a tunnel of sorts. Although it was dark, it was not pitch black. I passed by a pit where I could hear crying and moaning, but I did not stop to see what it was. I knew I was not interested.

I saw a light at the end of the hallway and a sheer curtain through which I could see people moving around. I wasn't afraid and I kept going toward them. When I got close, I asked why we had to have so many wars and killings on earth. Then I said, " I believe that Jesus was the Son of God. I believe in the Holy Ghost", but I could not remember the part about The Trinity.

Don't expect this part to make sense. It didn't make sense to me, but I'm repeating what happened to the best of my ability.

In a soft rhythm of threes, I heard what sounded like a train going over iron rails: *clickety-clickety-click, clickety-clickety-click.* Voices kept chanting over and over, "You live forever, you live forever, you live forever."

After what seemed a long time in the dark hallway, I cried out, "Oh, don't tell me there isn't any Heaven!"

Immediately a bright light filled the area where I stood. It was beautiful beyond description, so beautiful that it took my breath away. I'm not certain I can find the words to describe it, but I will try.

Standing in the light made me feel whole, pure, blessed, free

19

and loved. It was awesome. I wanted to bask in its energy and never leave. I felt I had just been born again into another realm, where I was completely at peace with my surroundings.

Again, voices told me that I would live forever and never die, that only my body would be left behind and that I would get a new body.

Three more things were revealed:

(1) There were no clocks in Heaven. My relatives would know when I was to arrive and, when I got there, it would be as if I had been with them always. This was impressed upon me as a very important fact. Only on earth do we feel the pain of separation. In Heaven, it was as if I was just one room away from relatives, friends, and family that I could see any time I wanted.

(2) There was no money or wealth to be brought with me, since it was of no value there.

(3) My position on earth was of no importance because I would be glorified in Heaven.

As I looked to my left I saw a curtain shaped like a steeple. It was closed at the top a nd open at the bottom. Again, I could see people moving about.

There was a darkened area that I would have to cross over, and somehow I knew that I would probably not come back to earth if I went through the curtained area. On one hand, I wanted to go ahead, and yet I hesitated.

I wanted to go back to earth and get Warren. I felt I needed to help him on his way to this beautiful place called Heaven. Warren had neuropathy in his legs and I was sure that he would need my help.

I knew I would be able to return to Heaven in the near future, so I told an Angel what I had in mind.

I didn't hear a reply, so I inquired if I could see my mother and father. I heard no reply then either.

When I asked if I could see Warren's mother. I heard a voice from behind the curtain say, "Thank you for the ball

20

and the cross."

I didn't know what that meant then, but I would understand it later.

I knew that the ability to see what I was witnessing was a great gift, and I also knew that I would never again have any fear of dying. What was waiting for Warren and for me was more than wonderful.

When I awoke in intensive care, I was watched very carefully, in case I slipped away again. After a couple of days, I awoke with a clear memory of what I had witnessed while out of my body.

I called my sister, Joy, and told her, "You had better get over here, because Mom and Dad and all your brothers and sisters will be coming". It seemed logical to me that if I could see Angels, she could also see them.

She hurriedly got dressed and came to the hospital. She told me later that, when she arrived, I was bubbly and happy. My niece and the nurse told Joy that I had awakened singing *Bringing in the Sheaves*.

Everyone said they could tell that I had indeed seen something wonderful. My face, they all agreed, was radiant. I told everyone who came to see me what I had seen and then I added, in a sing-song voice, "I've got a secret, I've got a secret."

I could not understand why I had been the one chosen to see this glorious sight, why I had been given such a gift.

You Live Forever, You Live Forever... / Gladys Hargis

3

Disappointing the Angel of Death

While I was in Intensive Care, I was still having problems. The doctors put a mirror down my throat then put me on oxygen and a B.I.P.A.P. machine to help my breathing. I was not exhaling carbon dioxide, and that was poisonous to my system. Also, when I collapsed, one lung had been punctured. Now it collapsed, causing me to die a second time.

There are no words to describe what happened next, but I'm going to say it to the best of my ability.

In another state-of-being, a woman, dressed in white dress, with gold pleated inserts in her skirt, showed me how to get out of bed in a way less painful to my back . She told me that her name was Mary, and that she had a nine-year old daughter.

Next, I was sitting in a marble room, talking to my husband Warren, my son Bill, and my daughter-in-law Tammy. I remember the room quite vividly, and a voice in the background chanting "You live forever, you live forever, you live forever."

I spoke to the Angels and asked them to explain to Joy that some Angels have wings, but that some do not.

Although I felt great peace with the Angels, this visit was very brief. I remember waking up back in my hospital room and hearing a doctors say, "That was a close call."

For the first time in my life, I understood that I had real knowledge. Important knowledge. I fully understood that I had

23

journeyed to another world, and that no one can enter until they are ready to die. As it turned out, I was not yet ready.

Later, when I was transported to a room on the sixth floor, I was still in a trance-like state, trying to grasp what it was I had just witnessed.

It was dusk when I awoke. A pretty nurse stood by my bed. When I asked her name, I thought she said, "Rose."

"Oh," I said, "you are the mother of Jesus."

She laughed and said, "No. You're still on earth."

That made no sense. After all, I'd just been in Heaven. Rose said that she was married to Michael, and that they had three children. I figured that Joseph had died and she married again. When I said as much, she continued to assure me that I was, indeed, back on this earth.

After we had talked for some time, a woman came from the back of the room and stood to one side. I could see her as plain as day. She was standing in what appeared to be some kind of alcove or extension, the kind you might find on a doublewide mobile home. The woman wore her hair in a short bob, and her dress was long and full, with those same gold pleats I had seen before.

She stood very quiet, as if waiting.

I told the nurse, Rose, there was a woman behind her, and Rose answered that she had seen her before, and I knew then that it was an Angel. I asked Rose what she thought the Angel wanted and Rose said the Angel was waiting for me. After a few seconds, the Angel turned, as if to leave—even though there was no door at the back of the room. The Angel of Death simply disappeared.

A couple of weeks later, a physical therapist came to exercise my legs. She told me that her name was Mary, and, recognizing her, I said, "Yes, and you have a nine year-old daughter."

She was surprise, as she had never met me before, and she wondered how I knew the age of her daughter. I told her

24

that I had met her when I was in ICU. She told me how that was not possible, as she and her daughter had just gotten home from California, where they had been for the past two weeks.

Yet, I had witnessed her ministering to me in ICU while I was outside my body. I had watched her wipe my brow. I knew her name was Mary and that she had a nine year-old daughter.

How or why I knew all of that so far ahead of actually meeting this Mary, I suppose we'll never know. Even I don't understand it.

I continued to improve and was to stay until Aug 30. I then was sent to the rehab hospital for eleven more days. When I called Rose to thank her for her care in the hospital, she told me that I had been given a great gift and that I had also been very, very sick, actually at death's door more than once.

You Live Forever, You Live Forever... / Gladys Hargis

4

The Ball and the Cross

Remember the ball and cross I mentioned earlier? Many months after my experience, my husband and I were going through some old letters written by his mother Esther, to her mother. One letter was dated early January 1929. In it, Esther thanked her mother and her sister, Minnie, for the gold crosses they had given her for Christmas.

Esther was pregnant, and was to deliver a baby in late July or early August. On July 29, she was accidentally shot and killed with a gun that was, supposedly, not loaded. It had been left out of its cabinet. When Esther's husband, Richard, picked it up to put it away, it went off. She was killed along with her unborn, full-term, daughter who was later named Emma Ruth.

When they were laid in the casket, the baby was wrapped in a blanket and put into her mother's arms. Around Esther's neck was a gold cross.

During visitation, an aunt, Julie, held Warren, who was two years old. In his hand was a litle rubber ball. Even that small, Warren remembers that he saw his mother in the casket and reached out to her. As he did, the little rubber ball slipped away from him and landed in the casket.

There was the explanation about the ball and the cross; his mother had on a gold cross, and the little rubber ball that belonged to Warren had been buried with her.

Warren and I both cried as we read the letter and understood the significance of what I heard Esther say, in Heaven, from

27

behind the curtain: "Thank you for the ball and the cross."

5

The Message That Brings Hope

I have told everyone what I saw and what I experienced. Even my doctor listened and thanked me for sharing it with him. He, in turn, shared it with his nurses and staff. He said that what I relayed to him would make him strive to be a better person.

Everyone I have told always expresses to me how wonderful it makes them feel to know what is to come. Some cry in relief, some cry for happiness, but it always brings a smile to their face and happiness to their heart.

I have given this message out to many friends and relatives. I have sent it to New Zealand, Ireland, and Germany. It is now being passed around the United States. Every day I am thankful to God for letting me see what is to come. I feel I am far richer than I would be if I won the lottery.

I wrote what would become the first draft of the first chapter of my book. At that time, I wasn't thinking about a book, I was only thinking about sharing my experiences. It was only about sixty pages. I sent them to four medical doctors, two of whom replied with notes of thanks. One doctor's wife had just died. He said that he could confirm my story with one of his own: He said he knew for a fact that his wife did not leave this earth alone, that someone came for her.

Another doctor sent me a letter saying that, after reading my story, he was inspired to leave his practice. He told his

29

mother that about the miracle I had experienced and then, inspired to do better with his life, he returned to his home state of New York where he went back to school and received a degree in an entirely new profession, one more dear to his heart.

6

Proclamation

Some people call what happened to me an out-of-body experience. I call it one of God's miracle mysteries.

After reading my story, it is my hope that everyone understands how earthly materials are of no value, only love *for everyone* is important. Genuine love of humanity cannot be bought, has no monetary value and is freely given; a gift more valuable than life itself.

Today, I have a feeling of excitement bursting inside me that makes me swell with pride when I think what a gift I was given, to be allowed a glimpse of the other realm. The excitement is there all my waking hours. With it comes enormous peace.

There is a wonderful trip ahead for all of us. Every one of our earthly chains will be taken away and our heavy load will be lighten.

Knowing that is the most glorious feeling on earth.

When you are able to accept it, you will understand that your Angel is near, every day of your life. But we must wait patiently for her to tell us when it is time to go.

You Live Forever, You Live Forever... / Gladys Hargis

7

Witnesses

My story has received rave reviews. Some people have had the same experiences I've had, but say I explain it in better detail. The nurse at the hospice said that he enjoyed my book very much and that I had been privileged to have witnessed what is to come for all of us. He also said that many of his patients saw what I saw before they left this earth.

He understood when I told him that I now realize that only our body dies, and that an Angel is with us before our final separation from our physical being.

There were times when I did not want to share all I saw, but pressure from beyond my understanding kept pushing me to tell it to the best of my ability. That is why I awoke from a deep sleep, singing "I've got a secret, I've got a secret". Everyone wanted to know what I had seen, and all I could do was beam and smile and sing.

It will all come out in God's time, I told myself.

Now is the time.

You Live Forever, You Live Forever... / Gladys Hargis

8

To Whom it May Concern

And so, my sixty pages have become this book about my Heavenly trip. I was encouraged by so many people to continue with my story. In particular, there was a doctor who knew that I had not told all there was to tell. He deals with patients who are on the threshold of that glorious place, and they have reported to him of seeing Angels. If anyone understands the truth of my story, it's him.

Because of all that happened, sometimes it is hard to know where to start and when to finish.

I am amazed that I saw so much in such a short period of time, and yet it all flashes back every now and then, assuring me that I will always remember it clearly.

As I've said, I saw Heaven, not just once, but at many different intervals. Since I was in intensive care for eight days, my life on this side was interrupted quite a lot.

I am not Catholic, but two priests, from Missouri and Kansas, praised me for telling my story, and encouraged me to continue.

You Live Forever, You Live Forever... / Gladys Hargis

9

Being Called to Witness

I do not know what "being called" means, but I have a burning desire to continue telling about what I saw when I made my trip to Heaven. As I said in the first chapter, in Heaven you can see everything with an open mind and a broad view, or clear understanding we lack at this earthly level. You take in so much that sometimes it is more in your subconscious than in your conscience mind. Yet, later, when you want to recall a feeling, or an observation, it is right there, at a moment's notice.

Besides the feeling of excitement, there is one of always being in awe. There is so much to tell. Even as I write this chapter, I am aware that I am skimming over some of my visions because I am limited by having to put it into words readily understandable.

Time has no meaning in Heaven. I was, literally, lost in time; it came to a complete standstill. I was free to wander along and take in all the sights.

The people who read the beginning of this book have asked all kinds of questions. Some wanted to know if there are both men and women in Heaven, and if you can you tell them apart.

The answer is yes. Men are usually dressed in a robe, where women are most often clothed in a dress that billows, like airy gossamer.

In Heaven, I asked for my mother and father. I saw them, but not in any way I would have anticipated.

My father, who had been married prior to marrying my

37

mother, appeared just inside the gate that led to a beautiful golden city. He walked slowly toward me, but stopped. I knew that he saw, and recognized, me, but he really no expression on his face except one of recognition. I also saw my mother, but she was behind him a good way. It was obvious they weren't together yet both had responded to my desire to see them.

My father was visible for only a few moments then he turned and walked to a door that opened into a building in the golden city. I remember wondering why my father was not with my mother and then it came to me that he would be with his first wife. They'd had a dozen children together, although he and my mother had another thirteen. In any case, I sensed no hostility between them and I knew, in my heart, that all was well.

I then asked an Angel if I might see Warren's mother, Esther. I was given a glimpse of her sitting just a few feet away. She was lounging on what I took to be a marble bench. She had dark hair and wore a dress that was light as air and floated around her. Seated next to her was a young blond girl I was certain was Emma Ruth, the unborn child who died from the same bullet that killed her mother.

Emma Ruth appeared to be somewhere between the ages of six and ten. Mother and child seemed happy and loving. I did not know either one of them when they were on this earth because they died in 1929 and I was not born until 1931.

Seeing Emma Ruth has led me to the conclusion there are no babies in Heaven. I think that, when a baby dies, the spirit leaves this earth as an older child, but I have no proof; that is simply my belief.

Cherubs might exist, as depicted in the Bible, but I did not see any..

What amazed me so was the love that spilled out from everyone I saw. I cannot repeat this enough.

Someone asked me about those who commit suicide. I

cannot tell you about that as the answers were not given to me, but my own understanding is that God wants you to live on His terms, and not end your life on yours. He did not promise that life would be easy for any of us. It seems that we are to struggle every day and take the good with the bad.

I feel that, if you love yourself and others, you will not end your life.

You Live Forever, You Live Forever... / Gladys Hargis

10

Explaining Heaven

In Heaven, you keep your own mind, your own consciousness just as it is on earth except that all ill feelings are gone. When I went through that white cloud everything negative was washed away. It was truly like being reborn, yet I knew who I was, I knew who my parents were, and who my friends were. I forgot nothing and yet everything was new, if that makes any sense whatsoever.

The feeling of love is so overwhelming that nothing else matters.

Someone asked if I recognized everyone I saw. The answer is yes. You will find that you can visit with your relatives and friends whenever you like, as they are always ready to appear at your request.

Since there is no such thing as time in Heaven, you will see people you have been separated from for a long while, yet, as I understand it, to them the separation is only an instant. This is another of those times it is hard to find words that accurately describe my meaning. When it happens to you, however, it will become crystal clear.

People ask if you work in Heaven, or is it all play.

When I was in the darkened hallway, you remember I tried to explain that I saw people moving things around. Later, when I told my husband about what I'd seen, he laughed and asked if they we removing cardboard boxes. I don't know what they were moving, but they were bent over, pushing objects around. I could not make out the objects so I concluded that the people were engaged in some sort of task that appeared to be quite effortless.

I'm often asked if we look the same as we look here on earth. The answer is yes and no.

You are not blood and muscle. You are as light as a feather, with a slim appearance. You look human. You have eyes, feet, hands, and you have hair on your head, but you do not walk, you simply float along.

You communicate through your thoughts. Replies are made through the thoughts of those you're "talking" to.

I was asked if you kiss or have sex. The answer is no. You remember your husband, but the sex on earth is a beautiful need of the physical body. In Heaven your body is beyond that kind of need. You get another kind of fulfillment from the love that flows between you and a loved one; it is a spiritual love. That kind of love satisfies you beyond your wildest dreams. There is no need to touch one another because you are touching them spiritually.

You will know your loved ones and enjoy their presence.

Someone asked me if it made any difference if they had been married more than once. The answer is no because you will visit and enjoy the best of every one.

If you believe in a loving God, and you are a good person, doing for others, loving others as you do yourself then, with God's blessings, I believe you will be able to experience the same things I have seen.

I believe that judgment occurs immediately after you close the door to this world. I know for a fact that if you are evil you will be judged. You will go straight to hell. When you go through that wonderful white cloud, and it washes your soul and makes you pure, you feel all the love that God has given you.

Why I saw hell, and heard the cries and moans, I do not know for certain. I feel now that it was so I could come back and tell everyone there is certainly a hell. If you are evil enough to go to hell, you will be there for all eternity.

The Lord has given me the ability to understand what I have witnessed, and I know that I am to spread the word of His workings, to tell everyone of the gift that is ours to come.

There are a lot of strange and wonderful things that are happening in our world, proof that there is a God, and that He is great.

You Live Forever, You Live Forever... / Gladys Hargis

11

Questions & Answers

When something happens to you as it happened to me, at first you will not be able to make any sense of it. I have asked numerous times. "Why me, Lord? What have I ever done to deserve this great honor?"

I now know that an Angel was with me long before I took what appeared to be my last breath. She continues to be with me even to this day. She is a part of me and of Warren, when he was with me. Some days it is hard to believe she is with me, but we accepted her as a blessing and a part of our home. She is my right hand, and guides me daily.

Warren had also seen her at the hospital, and he, too, sensed that she continued to be with us every minute. I am aware of her as she guides my thoughts so that I can help others who are going through the valley of the shadow of death, on their way to Heaven.

Sometimes she makes me get up at two or three o'clock in the morning because she doesn't know about clocks. She insists I tell everyone what is to come. She's very bossy! But I do her bidding. I get up and make notes so I won't forget to include them in this book, or the one I intend to write after the is one. She nags me not to forget things that happened to me.

At other times, she wants my attention in the middle of the day. For instance, I opened the garage door, but it kept going down by itself, so I opened it again and, again, it went down by itself. I gave up, went into the house and began writing down my thoughts and experiences while in Heaven. I was pretty certain that was what the garage door was all about because the next day, after I'd written pages and pages on my Heavenly journey, I went out to open it worked just fine.

I cannot tell you enough that when you leave this world, you will go into a beautiful new realm. It will bring you peace. It takes away all the chains of this world; they just fall aside. You do not realize how heavy those chains are until you get there and they drop away. Stress, anxiety and despair are no longer a part of your life. They are replaced by pure happiness, serenity and love.

That white cloud you initially walk through takes all the weight off your body and mind. You are left with good memories, and a mind that is sharp and filled with deep understanding. You do not remember yesterday but think only of the moment. You fill with such love, I can't even begin to explain it. It is so great, and so powerful, that it seems to flow from your very person onto others, then back around to everything and everyone.

Someone asked me if I was able to look down and see earth. No, but you don't even want to look back. You are so excited that you want to just look ahead and see what else is to come.

On one hand, I wanted to stay and take in the excitement, and bask in that incredible feeling of love. And yet I knew I would not be staying this time; that I would be back at a later date. Maybe because I was not in pain any longer. I did not mind returning; I had a job to do. I was to go back to earth and take care of Warren, who was very ill. There had been quite a discussion between Angles about whether I would be allowed to return or not, and it was decided I would.

Later, when I came to in my hospital room , my Guardian Angel appeared. She stood there so long, just waiting. I thought she was there to see if I was all right, or she might have been there in case I changed my mind about returning. I think that particular Angel really wanted me to come with her, but she accepted that I had a task to accomplish.

I can still feel her drawing power on me. I know that my time on earth is getting short. Warr en has gone ahead of me, and now I have this last job to do: I am to tell you—to convince and assure you—you that life is eternal and that God loves you very, very much.

You Live Forever, You Live Forever... / Gladys Hargis

12

Reincarnation and Wealth

Several people have asked me about reincarnation. There are a lot of questions I cannot answer because no answer was given to me. This is one of those questions I cannot answer.

There are some things I saw that, to this day, I still cannot describe, all I know for certain is that there is nothing to be afraid of. Let me repeat that: *do not be afraid.*

Everybody is here for a reason. Some people get their priorities mixed up. Some are selfish and desire wealth and comfort for themselves, while others have to struggle every day just to put food on the table and don't know, from one night to the next, where they will sleep.

I am convinced that God does not want you to starve, but He wants you to be willing to share the food you have with those who are without food. He wants you to have a roof over your head, but He also wants you to find a roof for others as well. He wants you to have clothes to wear, but He wants you to clothe other people, too. He wants you to have wealth, but He wants you to be willing to share your riches.

I use to struggle with the thought that I was not doing enough. I use to value my possessions. But, when I came back from Heaven, I realized that everything I own is of no value at all. It just collects dust, and is just for show.

If each of us would take just one person who has fallen on hard times and help them get on their feet again, help them

49

in make a living and supporting their families, and if they, in turn, would help someone else do the same, what a wonderful world this would be. It would fit into God's plan of having us love others as we love ourselves. An Angel told me that I could not bring wealth with me, that it had no value. That being the case, you you might as well put it to good use while you are on this earth. It will be left behind anyway.

I once knew a family who had great wealth. Before the father died, he made arrangements for his wife, three sons, one daughter, and himself, to be buried in copper caskets that costs $90,000.00 each. That amount of money would have fed ten families of four for over seven years. The man did give to orphanages, which speaks well of him, but the point is, he was still trying to take his wealth to Heaven.

13

God is Great

Some people tell me they do not want to leave their loved ones, and that is only natural. But your loved ones will be with you in Heaven. To understand this you must keep in mind that, in Heaven, time is not important. When you are ready to leave this earth, your loved ones who have gone ahead will come back to receive you. The ones left behind will be there with you before you even have a chance to miss them.

On the other side of the gate that separated me from Heaven's golden city, there was a beautiful garden. I never did go completely into the garden except for an occasional quick peek. All other times, I was on the outside looking in. I felt as if I were window shopping up and down the block. Since my return to earth I have heard others talk about their own visit to Heaven. Some have seen so much more than I saw, and yet I saw quite a lot.

I was able to communicate back and forth with those who were standing at the gate to my future home. Their invitation was very clear: I was welcome to enter—which I wanted very much to do—but discussions among the Angels were going on all the time I was standing there and I guess whoever was in charge knew my outcome better than I did. While I window shopped, I let them decide what was best.

Something exciting happens every second you are there. You may think that after you leave this earth you will lie in the grave, but that is so far from the truth. I want to climb up on my rooftop and, as loud as I can, shout to everyone that you don't have to worry. Since whatever pain you were in is taken away, you are able to work, your mind is free to experience what you see, and you have boundless energy.

It is light in Heaven. There is no darkness anywhere. I don't remember seeing any shadows, either.

I've been asked about flowers, but I cannot remember actual blossoms yet there was a beautiful garden. The surroundings are beautiful and colorful, though the colors are not any we have seen before. That's why I'm not certain if anything I saw in the garden could be classified as flowers. .

I keep trying to tell you about this place called Heaven. I cannot describe it to you accurately, though I continue to try.

There was a domed building on the far end of what I am calling a garden. I somehow knew it was the entrance into the Heavenly Kingdom, but, keep in mind, I did not go all the way in.

People want to know if I heard singing and beautiful music. I heard something like that, but the lovely sounds, like the incredible colors, blended into the surroundings. I liked what I heard; it seemed music-like, and yet it was actually more like chanting. Had I gone further into the garden, I am sure I would have heard more of the sweet sounding voices.

There is a good deal of curiosity as to whether only a few select people can go to this place I call Heaven.

In the Bible, God says that all are welcome *if* they believe in Him and if they repent. He tells us to go and preach His gospel, and to love one another as He loves us. There is room, He assures us, for everyone who comes to Him in faith. His Heavenly home goes on and on and on. It stretches out forever, in all directions. There is room for all of us and, I promise, you will be happy there.

As I write this, I'm thinking back to the time when I was

10 years old. We had a Sunday school project in my class where we were to read the Bible from cover-to-cover. The King James Version, New Testament, was easier for me to understand than other versions. I loved to read, and I read the Bible every chance I got, all that summer, into fall and on into the next summer. I would read in the hayloft, hiding up in the trees, in the back seat of our old car, in the outhouse—I'd even hide my Bible between the covers of the *Nancy Drew* mysteries, so my brothers wouldn't make fun of me.

I read the Bible from cover-to-cover, although it took two years. I found it to be a mystery, a tragedy, and a love story all wrapped into one. I wasn't so sure about the last book, called *Revelations,* though. That was too much for my young mind to take in, and it left me somewhat afraid.

I am happy that I spent my youth reading such an important book. I realize—especially since m my Heavenly journey—it is not only important book, it is a great book. God has now granted me the knowledge to understand His beautiful message.

When I started writing You Live Forever, my previous niece Helen was dying of cancer. She has since left us and I am at peace, knowing that she found God's outstretched hands waiting for her when she left to join Him. Her guardian Angel was sent to help her struggle through the separation from her body, and from this earth. Now she is perfect, healthy and happy.

Her brother, Duane, had left us at the age of forty, when his heart gave out. Her brother, Richard, died as an infant; her sister Patsy, father Dean; and her nephew Bryan were all there to receive her. I rest assured that she was escorted to Heaven's gates, where she, too, heard the chant: *You live forever, you live forever, you live forever.*

Believe me, for I know—God is, indeed, great.

You Live Forever, You Live Forever... / Gladys Hargis

14

In and Out of My Body

This story could go on forever and ever, just as the Heavens go on and on forever, but I want to share with you the seriousness of how I came back into this world from the other realm.

One thing I mentioned in the first part of this book was the mystery of how it all came about. I realized it had to be understood by my mind and my whole being in order for the trip to be truly worthwhile and for me to be able to tell it in a way you can accept. The gravity of the challenge was overwhelming.

Going back to how it all began, that day when I was rushed to the hospital, I could actually feel my body shutting down. I knew this was what it felt like to die, and that I was at my end of life on earth.

I drifted in and out of my body, as if time no longer existed. In this state, I looked around and saw a man standing in what I can only describe as his own space because my area of the emergency room was not that big. He stood quite straight and held a staff the way I imagined a shepherd watching his flock would hold one.

At first I thought he was a doctor dressed oddly and holding a saline bottle on a rolling staff, but upon closer inspection, I saw it was not so. His robe was off-white, with gold flecks in it. His hair was black and close-cropped. He was not looking at me, but was just standing as if he was listening. I even wondered if he might be guarding all of us in the room. And then I realized he was not of this world.

In Heaven, you are able to see everything in a wide swath, not like the tunnel vision of this earth. My observation of the man was made, not as a woman lying in a hospital bed, but from some other observation point. I was aware of doctors working over me and I could see that unearthly man standing there, watching, listening and waiting. I was told, much later, by my lung doctor, that everyone in the emergency room knew I was on the brink of death. He said that my organs were shutting down. They took a chance and gave me heavy doses of insulin. It worked, but it took its own sweet time.

Meanwhile, I was in Heaven, talking to Angels at the gate. Amazingly, I saw the man from the emergency room standing in the garden, to my left. He was not looking directly at me, but was still listening while watching what was going on around him. The shepherd's staff was in his right hand, while in the hospital room it had been in his left hand. It seemed odd that I would notice the difference. I think I was trying to establish whether it was real or simply a dream. Even as I questioned it, I knew it was real.

Warren said later that, while he was in my hospital room, he, too, saw the man with the staff . Keep in mind that while we were seeing this male being, I also saw a female Angel. I came to realize that the male Angel was with me throughout my travels in the other realm.

I've been asked if I thought he was God, and I've said I did not think so. And then I'm asked if it could have been Jesus. I do not think so even though it was impressed on me that Jesus will be at our side when we end this journey and travel into Heaven.

15

Joy Beyond Description

The most amazing thing about this part of the story deals with my understanding of wha t happened when I returned to my body.

When they put oxygen and an air pack on my face, my brain went through a transformation of some sort. I can only compare it to the defragmentation of computer files and folders. I could "see" the building blocks of my brain in shades of red, yellow, blue and green, re-stacking into piles. I did not think it would ever end. It continued until I finally fell asleep.

When I awoke, many hours later, I felt as if I had been born again. My mind took on new knowledge of what I had witnessed—and experienced—away from my body. I knew I had been given a gift from Heaven and from our Lord. It was instilled in me that I was of very sound mind, more alert, more knowledgeable than I had ever been before, with full understanding of what I had witnessed. I also knew, without any doubt, that I would never forget what I had experienced. I would carry the memory until I returned to my Heavenly home.

It was at this point, I died again and I left my body for the second time.

I heard a doctor say to the male nurse, "She will more than likely have some brain damage. She may not even recover."

Even though I was unconscious, I saw a nurse shake his head, indicating that he understood.

All this time, they were attempting to resuscitate me. All toll, I stopped breathing three times during my long ordeal. Each time, I returned with my mind as clear as a bell, with no outside influences clogging my brain. Every evil, or negative, thought, and every bad memory, was gone.

Today I am a new person, in tune with God's love and with love for everyone. Nothing else matters.

This most wonderful experience has changed my life forever. There is never any anxiety or fear now. My belief in a Higher Being has always been there, but to see and feel it so vividly is astounding. Sometimes I am so giddy with happiness about what I saw on the other side that I want to hurry and return.

I loved, and still love, my husband and my family, and I have enjoyed my life, but I am also getting old. I realize that my return to Heaven is closer than I might think. Closer than any of us realize.

I hope that, through this book, I have been able to bring you a firm assurance that all is well with the Lord, if you live your gift of life to the fullest with love, as God wants you to do, and if you understand that you are to love everyone as yourself.

16

Angels Abound

The Angel who is with me in my daily life will have to send me a clear signal about what I need to do with all this information. I know I saw quite a bit more on my trip to Heaven than I can describe, but I simply can't think how to tell about it. Some of the things I saw are beyond description. I have faith that she will let me know in due time. Maybe she already has. Maybe that's why I'm writing a second book even as I complete this one.

Even though I want to hurry and leave this earth, she tells me, in no uncertain terms, that I am not to try to go ahead of my time, that we are all on this earth for a reason, and we are to go about our lives remembering that we are God's children, and that we will answer to Him, and do as He asks. There are a lot of good works still to be done, and we are meant to find what they are and do them in God's name.

Life is so precious. We aren't meant to just stand by and watch the poor, the sick and the desperate, starve, struggle, and weep in despair. We need to love them and ease their suffering. Every act of kindness transforms the world around us.

You Live Forever, You Live Forever... / Gladys Hargis

17

Miracle in August

I have held off telling everyone details about the city I saw. It was such an amazing sight that it was almost too much to take in. It was such a marvel I wasn't sure anyone would believe me. I felt I had witnessed something secret, and that only the Angels and I shared that particular gift from the Heavens.

Now I realize now that I am to share that "secret" with you.

While there is no such thing as time in Heaven there is distance. I saw the Heavenly city when I came out of the cleansing white cloud. It was set far off, maybe two miles away.

After my recovery, when I was trying to tell Joy about what I saw, she asked if there were skyscrapers or bridges. There were not. The entire city was nestled close to what we would call ground. A lot of the buildings were domed, with golden colors: white-like ivory and pearls, and gray-like marble. It was the way the city sparkled and shone in the light that left me nearly breathless.

It seemed to be spread over many miles. I feasted on its beauty for some time, realizing that this was what I will have when I return again from earth. The very fact that it exists, assures me that all will be well for all of us, that we will never miss what we had on this earth, and that we will never want to come back to earth once we are in Heaven.

After you have reading this book, it is my prayer that you will be as happy as I am, just knowing what God will be giving to you as well.

I will have to wait patiently now for the Angels to remind me of the many more things I am to tell you. When I begin with a new chapter, you will know that I have been nudged to continue and that my Angel has allowed me to remember even more that I am to share.

.

18

Loved Ones Await

This chapter is really a recap of the previous six chapters, to try to fill in what I might have missed, and to remind you of the important things I was shown and am to share with you.

In looking back, and putting the pieces together, I feel that after you go through the white cloud, and your soul is cleansed, you, too, will see that beautiful city in the distance.

You will have to go through a filmy curtain then pass through the garden gate. Your friends and relatives will be there to welcome you in. After that, you will go through the domed building and into the Eternal City.

As I said earlier, the Eternal City is way beyond the garden, but yet you will have the ability to see it in the distance, gleaming in the light.

You will glide everywhere.

From what I saw, I am absolutely certain that what lies beyond the city must be more than wonderful. Treasures beyond our wildest dreams.

It is then you will understand that nothing here on earth is of any value.

You Live Forever, You Live Forever... / Gladys Hargis

19

The City, The Gate

Dreams are a part of our earthly life, but I knew what was happening to me was not a dream. I was separated from my body and looking back at what was going on around me on earth. I was past feeling any pain, and yet I knew the medical staff was prodding me and sticking needles in my body. They were also using paddles, trying to make me respond.

The incidents that I describe here are branded into my memories. They will be with me for all eternity.

I know when I return to that Heavenly place, I will recognize and remember everything I saw, and I will know that I have been there before.

I knew, each time I took in all the sights, that time was endless, and yet I knew I did not have time to tarry. My mind was like a sponge, soaking in everything around me.

I have not yet mentioned that other people were there, at the gate, but they were. They looked familiar and yet I coule not then, nor can I now, put a name to them. They were excited that I was there, and I knew they wanted me to come in. They were happy and laughing, and they emitted lots of love toward me. Even at that, I realized it was not my time to enter the gate and so I looked beyond them.

The first building past the gate, and beyond the curtain, was a huge structure made of granite. It had large openings for windows. Oddly enough, I noticed there were no screens. Everything was open, with no obstructions. There were wide

open doorways, but no doors that shut.
    I took time to marvel at the domes of shimmering ivory.
The Eternal City was further off in the distance.

20

Earthly vs Heavenly Body

Another frequent question is whether or not shoes are worn in Heaven, and all I can say is that I did not see any. I actually did not need them because my feet never touched whatever the brownish area below my feet was made of. You float from here to there, yet you move your legs. I say that and yet the male Angel I saw later was walking in the garden, clearly on a path.

I have been asked about glasses.

You take in everything with your mind, but you have eyes and you see out of them as we do here on earth. You look like a human being, but with so many improvements, it's difficult to describe.

People want to know about food, but I did not experience what the Bible refers to as a "feast at the banquet table" where all your relatives gather. Maybe that happens once we are inside the Eternal City.

I was not told how or what the body is made of, or how it works. All I know is that you are as light as a feather, and you just glide right along. I did notice how light you feel there, without the chains of life you have to carry here on this side.

As you read and, hopefully, enjoy this book about my trip to Heaven, I hope I have explained it well enough that you will come to understand I was only given a peek into what is to come for all of us.

Every day you must thank God that He has prepared a

home for us. Our old bodies were created to wear out, but our new "body" will last forever.

21

Angels Never Leave Us

I T is amazing to know that Angels are with you from the beginning to the end of your journey. They welcome you in song and rejoice with an outpouring of love.

You never feel alone or afraid. You are drawn to their power, and yet they only guide you. You want to follow them because the love they give you is so overwhelming.

I never saw any Angels with wings, but I would not be surprised to find some.

I did notice that the one male Angel I saw was very serious. Of course, I only saw that same one twice that I remember. There were several female Angels. They were very friendly and excited, ready to welcome me into their fold.

Love is everywhere, and it draws you into everything.

The people I saw at the g ate were not Angels, and the fact I knew the difference surprised me. Even the ones I saw at the end of the hallway, moving things around, I don't think were Angels.

The people I saw at the gate were beckoning me to come in. I still see them in my mind and someday I feel it will come to me who they are.

There was a man standing outside the gate and away from the women. He smiled as if he knew me. That's when I realized God had wanted me to know who they were, someone would have told me.

69

Something happened that confused me terribly. It had to do with Mary, the Mother of Jesus. I am aware that, at some point, I had been talking to her, but I could not remember what it was about. I could not get it clear in my head. I remember that I was surprised that she wanted to converse with me, because I am not Catholic. I didn't think of then, but later I realized that Mary is not Catholic either. She is the mother of Jesus, but more importantly, she is the mother of all.

When I regained consciousness in the Intensive Care Unit, I asked the nurse if she was Mary, mother of Jesus. She smiled and said she was not, yet I can remember clearly that I saw Mary earlier, sitting on a smooth stone bench in Heaven, smiling. Thinking I was still in Heaven, I was certain that dear lady at my side was Mary.

Warren said the line on the monitor went flat several times, then alarm bell would go off, the Code Blue light would sound and everyone would come running. He said it had happened so many times that the staff quit asking him to leave.

My bed was located next to the nurse's station. They asked Warren if he wanted a minister to call on me. Warren was trying to prepare himself for what was to come. He told me later that he could feel an unseen presence during my near-death experience. He knew that Angels were watching over all of us.

I feel certain there are always Angels in the ICU area, and that they never leave.

22

Secrets

I did not want to come back to earth for my own gain or loss. I wanted to come back to help Warren so he could come with me to that beautiful realm. However, I was ready and willing to stay, if that was what was expected of me.

I wished I'd had a conversation with my mother and father while I was there. It remains something that I cannot grasp. I know I saw them, but when I think back, that part of my experience is vague.

Some people say they would like to see their mother again, and I say, "Look in the mirror". Many times when I do that, I can see my mother looking back at me. I enjoy it because I am able to convey my thoughts to her. She was a very good Christian lady and a loving person. She guided us, with the help of Angels.

I wake up happy and go to bed happy, knowing what I know.

I do, indeed, have a secret. At least I had one until I realized I was to write this book.

You Live Forever, You Live Forever... / Gladys Hargis

23

Our Home Awaits

Every time I woke up from my hospital bed, I found someone nearby hoping that I would be able to tell them something more. Even my minister said he understood my sightings, and he believed they were true. He agreed that I had witnessed something remarkable.

I could not believe that I had been so blessed.

All who came into my room left convinced that something marvelous was happening, and it was a miracle that I was alive to tell it.

My heart and my voice sang out constantly. My happiness was overwhelming, and it left me almost breathless, though my breathing machine took care of most of that.

Thank you, God, for letting me see and tell what is to come for all of us.

Every day we must all thank God that He has prepared such a home for all of us.

You Live Forever, You Live Forever... / Gladys Hargis

Family Album

Gladys' parents, George & Hattie Thompson (1942)

Karl & Thekla Kuglin with daughter Margaret, taken in Africa

Hattie Thompson with Gladys' brother, baby Carroll, who died when he was 7.

Warren and Gladys Hargis

75

You Live Forever, You Live Forever... / Gladys Hargis

PART II

True Stories of Miracles in Our Life
with Angels and Christian Love

You Live Forever, You Live Forever... / Gladys Hargis

24

Mother's Visit

W arren and I had many miracles in our married life. I
never took any of them for granted.

Warren's Uncle Karl was a missionary in Nigeria,
Africa where he lived with his wife Thekla. On November 17,
1943, at 6:30 in the evening, they were hoeing their garden.
Thekla said she was about twenty- five feet away from Karl
when she heard voices. She thought someone had come to visit.
When she looked up from her weeding, she saw that Karl was
smiling and appeared to be talking to someone even though
there was no one else in sight.

Thekla called out, "Who are you talking to?"

Karl replied, "My mother."

Thekla arose and went to him. His face was beaming; he
was smiling and happy. She could not see anyone around, yet
the great smile on his face was enough to tell her that he was
seeing someone and feeling the presence very much alive in the
U.S.

Later, when they went back into the house, they talked about
what had happened and they thanked God for such a gift, though
they couldn't under the significance.

It took six weeks for mail to reach Africa from where
Karl's mother lived, in Holton, Kansas. When Karl received
their next mail delivery, he learned that his mother, Elizabeth,
had passed away on November 17, 1943, at 6:30 in the evening
Nigerian time.

You Live Forever, You Live Forever... / Gladys Hargis

25

My Brothers and Their Angel

The story about Karl and his mother reminds me of when my brother Lee died. Dying was a blessing for him because he had a rare form of infectious rheumatoid arthritis. He was bedridden and in severe pain.

The day the Angel came for him, I was sitting beside his bed, talking to him. It was late afternoon. While I was looking at him, I noticed a veil come over his eyes. Where a moment before they had been watery, they were now dull, with no life in them. He was still breathing, but I knew his time was short.

I had never seen anything like it. I have asked several ministers and doctors why this happened, but they had never witnessed such a thing for themselves and could not answer.

I knew, because I could sense it, that someone was there with Lee, someone I could not see. I knew it by the way he seemed more at peace and at rest.

Five months later, I lost another brother, Mark, to lung cancer. He lived in West Virginia. I traveled with my sisters and family to see him in his last days. The night before we left, I went into his room to say my goodbyes. Although he was alone, he was smiling and talking to someone I could not see. I asked who he was talking to and he smiled and said, "Lee is here and getting impatient. He said to hurry up as he has things to do and places to see." Then Mark added, "I can hardly wait for the Angels to take me. I wish they would hurry."

81

You Live Forever, You Live Forever... / Gladys Hargis

26

Changing Churches

Warren had been raised in the Evangelical church, and I was brought up as an American Baptist. We were married in his church and stayed with his religion for our first years of marriage.

Since both churches led to God, it made no difference to us which one we attended. Warren's Uncle Karl and Great Uncle Christopher were both ministers of the Evangelical church and were a guidance in his life. He and I had known Christ all our lives so, between the two of us, we had the best of both worlds.

We moved to Topeka and settled in the Evangelical United Church. When our son, Bill, was born we soon found out that he would not have brothers or sisters. Warren and I decided to take foster children into our home. This was a miracle for all of us. It gave Bill playmates and it gave the other children a loving home.

While attending the Evangelical church, we found that something was lacking in our lives. Warren was a city fireman. He would work a few days in a row then have days off, so he took to building houses in his spare time. We had built a large house for our family, in the country.

One day, as he was driving down the street, he noticed a small Baptist church that looked like it needed some help with painting, mowing the large yard, and carpentry work. He came home and asked if the family wanted to go to another church for a while. It sounded like fun, and we all attended the Baptist church the next Sunday. Despite the great reception, Warren said he needed to pray about

83

making a change before he joined for good.

One night, months later, Warren woke up suddenly. He was used to waking up at odd times of the night because, when he was on duty at the firehouse, he slept in the watch office. Thinking he was at the fire station, he arose and, looking out of the window by our bed, he saw a man sitting on a rock in the garden, about twenty feet away. The man wore a robe with a hood and was smiling.

Warren, now fully awake, realized it was his Uncle Karl. Warren was so surprised. He called for me to come and see. When I got up and looked out the window, I could not see Karl, but, judging by the look on Warren's face in the moonlight, I knew he had seen his uncle.

27

Our Family Miracles

We had been attending the small Baptist Church for some time when, one day in Sunday school, we got into a discussion about belief in God. Was the Bible really real, or was it fiction written for the times? Was there really a God after all?

We all agreed that we needed to test the theory of God's existence. We were a bit skittish about this testing so, when I prayed, I asked for just a little miracle, not a big jolt, but just a little nudge to prove to me once and for all that He did indeed exist.

I had been read to and preached to all my life, and I wanted to believe in everything, but I just needed a little reassurance.

My children knew this had been discussed, and they seemed to have more faith than I had as they warned me that something terrible would happen. Maybe the world would end, their house would burn down, or God would get mad and strike me down and then they would not have a mother.

We promptly forgot about the idea of testing God.

Several months later, Warren and I decided to take the family to our Aunt Minnie's farm in Holton for Sunday dinner. Because it was forty miles north, we decided to skip church and get an early start.

It was a beautiful day. The sun was shining and there was not a cloud in the sky. Driving along, we discussed the fun we would have that day on the farm.

After about forty-five minutes, we stopped at the family cemetery to check on the graves of Warren's relatives, including his mother, Esther, Esther's unborn daughter Emma, his grandparents, and his father. We then continued on.

About one mile from the farm, all of a sudden, from out of nowhere, the sky started getting terribly dark and wind buffeted our truck. Warren could not keep it on the road, and he was afraid it would overturn. It got even darker in a very short time, and we knew we could not travel the last distance to our aunt's home.

We pulled into the driveway of a neighboring farmhouse and, with some effort, ran for their back porch to take cover.

There were cars about yet, after repeated knocking, we could not get anyone to answer the door. It was unlocked, so we went in and found ourselves on their glassed-in back porch. Grateful for the shelter, we kept yelling for someone to answer us, but to no avail.

I saw through the glass inset in the back door that food was cooking on the gas stove. Flames were licking up, almost engulfing the frying pan. Fortunately, that door was also unlocked. I was afraid that the handle on the frying pan would catch fire, so I hurried into the kitchen and turned the flame down very low.

I continued to shout for someone to answer us, but no one did. We wondered if the owners were maybe in the basement, waiting out the storm and were afraid to answer when they heard the tromping of twelve feet on their porch. We must have sounded like cattle had gotten loose in their house. Still, I did not think they would have forgotten their potatoes frying on the stove.

When the winds began to quiet down, we left and drove on to our aunt's place .

When we got to the lane that our aunt's farm was on, the sky turned blue again and we saw Aunt Minnie coming from the chicken house.

The children were all excited and asked Minnie if she was frightened by the storm. She seemed surprised by the question. She said she had been out feeding the chickens and there was no storm around. The sky, she had noticed, was a beautiful blue, and clear as a bell.

She was only one-half mile away from her neighbor and would have noticed the dark clouds.

Warren chimed in with the children, who were berating me for testing God. They let me know they were not happy, and, in fact, to this day they have never let me forget it.

The children and Warren made me promise that I would never again ask for a sign.

I thank God that He sent a storm at just the right moment for us to seek shelter which led, in turn, to us saving that family and their farmhouse from a deadly fire.

God is everywhere. We don't need to test Him, but when we do, He lets it be known we are not alone.

You Live Forever, You Live Forever... / Gladys Hargis

28

God Has a Plan

God and his Angels have a plan for the life of all of us. Whether you like it or not, it follows you wherever you go. Now that I am growing old, and looking back, I can see the plan much more clearly than ever before.

Warren and I had wanted a big family and we soon had exactly that. We were never sorry we opened our home up to all of our foster children.

Our first child, Bill, was a special gift. He was everything anyone could wish for, a bouncing, blue-eyed, baby boy who was our little miracle. The second, third, fourth, fifth and sixth ones were neighborhood children we helped get through their kindergarten years, to their teens. They had their own parents to go home to at night. They have remained our friends.

However, God wasn't through with us yet. He had a bigger plan in store.

*

We decided to take in children who would not leave us at nightfall. This changed our life considerably.

We took a family vacation every year, to learn about other people, and animals, and the wonderful land that God gave us to enjoy. We have never regretted taking the additional children into our home. They have grown into wonderful adults, and have families of their own. We have been rewarded with

eight grandchildren, and five great-grandchildren.
 What an enjoyment and a miracle.

29

Christian Fun

I don't want you to think that just because you go to church, you cannot have fun, because that is not so. We had a lot of fun attending both Sunday school and church.

We often got together for meals with our church family.

Together we planned and painted the outside of the church, and repaired some of the brickwork. We assigned adults and children to clip weeds and keep the extra large lot mowed. Then we set about getting other families in the area to come and join us.

We sold candles one year to make extra money so we could buy and put down a carpet in the church entryway. The ladies had a garage sale that was lots of fun. It lasted for two days and on the second day, thanks to a student from the Kansas University, we were able to get rid of nearly everything. We gave him a small table, one lamp, a kitchen chair, some dishes, an easy chair, and other assorted items for free.

He was driving a Volkswagen and he couldn't see how he could get it all in his tiny car. But never fear when Christians are at work. The Angel showed us how we could do it.

We removed the backseat and put all the stuff in the empty space. It took some packing and rearranging, and then we roped the car seat to the top of his Volks. We took a picture of it because we could not believe we had accomplished such a task.

All of us, including the young man, prayed that God would let him get back to his dorm safely, and then we sent him merrily down the road.

We closed the garage sale because everything was gone. We never heard from the student again, but we trust the Angels that he reached home safely.

He felt good for having received such a bounty, but we felt even better for giving it.

30

A Stranger Among Us

Several times we took all the children, and some of their friends, to Worlds of Fun in Kansas City. One time we started home with one too many little boys.

We had counted heads, but another one of my group got into the wrong car, and I did not know it. So I had the right count, but a wrong child—another little boy joined our group and was having so much fun he didn't want to leave us. I only discovered the child when someone mentioned it after we were already on the road. We had to turn around and take him back to Worlds of Fun and his worried parents.

The exchange was made and, after we got the children switched, I had everyone identify themselves and vouch for each other before I left the park again. Some of the children's friends were strangers to me, so the mistake was easy to understand, but I still shudder to think how close we came to inadvertently kidnapping a little boy.

The next year, we drove all the children and their friends to Summer Retreat in Colorado. We played campfire games, sang songs, went on hikes in the mountains, slept in cabins, and learned how God plays a part in our daily lives.

You Live Forever, You Live Forever... / Gladys Hargis

31

Christmas Pageant Joy

Every year, for seven years, we put on a Christmas nativity scene at church. Now that was a treat. It made everything worthwhile.

We hunted around and found a very gentle donkey from one of the daycares in town. The men from the church had built a stable, and we built a manger and got some hay and straw from the farms. Then we built a bonfire and strung lights.

We borrowed two sheep from a farmer, an ewe and her lamb. We needed the help of all our children because the sheep were another story entirely. If you have ever been around sheep, you will understand when I say that they went everywhere but where we wanted them to go. We had to lift the mother up, once we caught her, and carry her to the bed of the truck. The lamb was sure to follow. Loading them up to take them home was also a challenge, but we had strong men around to help.

The sheep never did get the idea to run into the bed of the truck when we went after them. They would run all over the place no matter what we wanted them to do. Every year, my children looked forward to trying to catch them. We would laugh for days afterward. I imagine the Angels were laughing as well. Next year, however, the children were ready to go again to help out.

We were spoiled by the gentle nature of the donkey so, the second year, we weren't ready for what was to come. We had to switch to a wild, stubborn, one the following year, and we had great difficulty getting him loaded. This, again, took help om the Angels, after all, we can accomplish everything with their help. In the end, we needed, not only our Angels, but a long stick, a halter, and a very long carrot.

We used the wild donkey for several years, and we think he finally got the idea of what his job was at Christmastime. He began waiting for us by the gate, however, without the carrot, he still did not like the truck.

One of the ladies who had a friend in the Shriners found they had some old long velvet gowns that members of their organization had worn for ceremonies. They wanted to get rid of them, so we took them and they worked out great.

The wise men were dressed in finery

We performed outdoors for five nights, though some nights it was very cold. We all relied on a bonfire to keep us warm and toasty.

Warren, as I said earlier, was a fireman for the city, so he was in charge of watching the bonfire, to keep it safe and keep us warm. The adults and the children enjoyed our efforts, and it brought the meaning of Christ's birth and His Angels to them.

My children still, to this day, remember that time in our lives, and wish their children could experience the same thing. Times have changed for them, but they are happy doing their own things, creating their own memories with their own children.

And I remember, too, that they each have their own Guardian Angel, and they are living out God's special plan.

32

My Father and His Angel

My father, George, was raised in a Christian home, but he had been orphaned at the age of three. His father was a deacon in his church, and was a widower with four children to raise. He needed to remarry and have a wife to help him take care of his family.

My father was the youngest born to Carroll and Charity Thompson, in 1872, just about six years after the Civil War. He was born in a small settlement called Spirit Mound, near Vermillion, South Dakota.

His father, two brothers and one sister, drove the team and wagon to town to buy supplies. His mother, Charity, along with my father, who was a baby at that time, was left at home.

Charity heard shouting from far away, and when she looked out the window, she saw Indians coming toward the farmhouse. She was very frightened, but she found her courage and gathered up my dad.

Being careful not to be seen, she let the animals out of their pens and slipped down to the creek where she got into the water and hid under a large hollow tree stump. She nursed my father to keep him quiet. She told her husband later that she could see the bare feet of the Indians, walking along the edge of the creek, searching for her.

Even though she was cold, she stayed until it was dark and then she crept out of the water and returned to the house. She could not start a fire to get dry for fear of the Indians being close at hand, so she sat awake in a chair all night until her husband returned the next morning.

God was looking after them. It was a miracle they survived.

After that, Grandfather Carroll sold their home and moved his family back to Alton, Illinois. Grandmother Charity was never well after that. When she died, it was believed that the cause was being out all night, nursing my father in the cold water.

My grandfather kept the older children and gave his sister, Caroline, my father to take care of.

Carolina was Catholic. She kept George until he was about six, and then George went back to live with his father and his father's new wife Jennie, who was born i n Switzerland and spoke broken French.

They saw that George had the opportunity to attend college in Alton, Illinois where he studied French and art. He was a great painter of portraits and was skilled at sketching. He also took up wallpapering and house painting. He was well known as the artist who painted the Angels and cherubs in the high ceilings of the train station and churches in Alton.

My dad's brother, Anso, was seven years older, and was murdered at the age of fifteen while helping to feed hoboes down at the river's edge in Alton . His body was never found, but the man who murdered him was caught. He was given a life sentence and died in the federal prison in Leavenworth, Kansas.

My father was nearly twelve when Anson was killed. It changed Dad's life, and caused him to be restless and unsettled. Despite that, he was a good student and continued with his studies. He was seventeen when he finished college. He traveled extensively, working on a ranch in Arizona, breaking horses and herding cattle.

Dad had a friend of long-standing traveling with him. Dad drew up plans for a table, with a wheel in the middle, that held sugar, salt and spices. His best friend stole Dad's plans and made lots of money. He never gave my father any credit or any money for the invention. From then on, my Dad never gave away any of his ideas, and he had many.

At the age of twenty-two, he married his cousin. After seven children and a troubled relationship, they called it quits.

In February 1917, at the age of forty-five, he met and married my mother, Hattie. At the age of sixteen, my mother was told by a doctor that she would never have any children. So she put the idea of marriage out of h er mind and stayed home to care for her ailing mother.

My mother was twenty-nine years-old when she met my father, who had come to their house to decorate and paint it. He was smitten with her and delighted that she could not have children. With seven of his own, he did not need any more. Hattie and George decided they would spend their life touring the world, but God had other plans..

My dad could do just about anything to make money, so supporting his new wife was not going to be a problem while they traveled. He had been a painter, a motorcycle police officer, a contractor, a farm hand, and a ranch hand. He thought he had the world at his fingertips. However, in December 1917, Carroll, his first son with my mother, was born in Shenandoah, Iowa. So much for well-set plans.

In 1919, Margaret was born in Oregon. She died three weeks later. Another daughter was born in 1920, in Georgia. In 1922, son Lee was born in Texas, and another son, Mark, was born in 1923 in Asheville, North Carolina. It was in Ashville that Carroll got sick and died. Daughter Joy was born in 1926 in Topeka, Kansas, and son John was born in 1927 in Olympia, Washington. Finally, I was born in 1931, in Benton, Arkansas. To let you know that God does have a sense of humor, we were all born in different states. My parents had great souvenirs from their travels.

99

My father was fifty-nine years old when I was born. I think he had been praying for the population explosion to end for many years. God finally did answer him in 1931.

My father had a lot of sins to resolve by this time, but God and his Angels were still looking out for him and gave him a sign, though it was a while in coming. Meanwhile, he joined the Odd Fellows and the Masons. They were secret societies, but it is my understanding they study the Bible and believe in God. I was always listening around the doors and through keyholes to find out what they were about, but my parents seemed to know when ears were listening, and they would just talk softer. I finally gave up.

My father and mother always saw that we attended church from the time we arrived on this earth. We could only miss Sunday school and church if we were sick. My father did not attend Sunday church, but he and my sister went together on Wednesday nights. Dad was like a guardian angel, always watching out for us, always trying to keep us on the straight and narrow. None of my brothers ended up in jail, but I am told they did get scolded by police officers several times. If it looked like one of them might be heading the wrong direction, they were encouraged to enlist in the navy the next day.

All of them served their country without getting killed in the war. They married and raised families, so my mother and father had a lot to be thankful for.

My mother was a saint in her own right, and I am sure my, father, before his death, resolved his issues and got things straight with God and his Angels.

On the night my father died of cancer—December 16, 1949, when I was eighteen years of age—my mother and I tended to him at home. We soothed his mouth with ice cubes, to take away some of the pain. He said that Angels were coming for him.

He said he saw an Angel dressed in white,

standing on a platform on the back of a train. He heard a whistle and knew it was time to go. The train was going down tracks that crossed our land about a quarter of a mile away. We listened but could not hear the whistle. The tracks had been abandoned many years before. They were broken and rails were missing.

My mother and I went to stand by the window, and we saw a ray of light, large enough to fit on the front of a train, waving back and forth, gas if it were going down the tracks. We then heard what sounded like a whistle. We could not understand what we saw because there were no explanations. There were only farm fields and grazing land around the tracks.

My mother and I checked in town the next morning, to see if the tracks had been repaired, but they were still broken up. A man at the all-night gas station said that he also heard a train whistle far off in the distance, late in the evening. He, too, was surprised to hear the sound.

My father left us a short time later, with the broadest smile on his face. He seemed to glow, knowing where he was going and who he was going with. To witness this, even though I was sad at his leaving, I knew he was with the Lord, and that the Angels were taking him home.

I learned that night that we had just borrowed him for such a short time.

What a miracle.

You Live Forever, You Live Forever... / Gladys Hargis

33

God and His Angels

Our small Baptist church was not growing as we would have liked it to. We were able to get lots of children to come, but their parents would drop them off and then go back home. We tried several things to encourage the adults to attend as well, but we could see it was going to be an uphill battle. This battle had been going on for a long time, but we all thought we could make a difference. The bigger churches were drawing in the adults because they were more bigger and more beautiful. They also had more money to work with.

We suffered a set-back when we began to lose a lot of our older members. Some went on to Heaven, and some to other churches. We should have been able to see the handwriting on the wall, but our family did not want to give it up. We tried everything we could think of. We sent out flyers and put up posters. Then we lost our minister and his wife, who moved back east to continue their education so they could become teachers. We were then without a full-time leader. We finally had to concede that God had other plans in mind and we would have to change our plans accordingly.

Warren was a deacon and was saddened that we would have to close down our church and move somewhere else, or merge with another church.

We became members of the First Baptist Church, which had one thousand members. Our son Bill and his wife Tammy were married in that church, which made us proud.

It also gave us a chance to rest for a year and re-build our energies. We look ed back and realized that we could not have done anything without the help of God and His Angels. I don't understand how anyone can live without a firm belief in God.

I had a chance to go to Green Lakes, Wisconsin for a seminar with other Christians. I think God was giving me a chance to rest and enjoy other people.

When I came back, Warren and I were made head of the local missions.

God gave us rest and then He gave us the strength to begin a new phase of our life, doing His work.

34

The Heavens Open Up

My sister Joy told me, the night her husband Dean died, that he was lying in bed and that it was just after midnight. They knew he was pretty sick, and had been for some time. Dean did not want to see a doctor. He refused to have a physician look at him.

Joy was sure he had cancer because he was in so much pain. But he still refused to go, and said he had a right to die at home if he wanted to. Besides, he agreed with her theory about cancer, and felt it had gotten too much of a head start, and had gone too far. He knew for sure that he did not want to die in a hospital.

All of his family was trying to help him as best they could, but he refused their help. They still would come in and out most of the day, to check on him. He was sleeping almost all the time and there was nothing they could do but give him pain killers.

Joy had to continue working since their only income was hers.

On the night Dean died, Joy came home and parked the car in the garage. She brought several things into the house, then returned to close the garage door. Before she did that, she noticed a single bright light, like a streak of fire, shooting up from the roof, over the room where her husband was sleeping. It shot up and then rose up, into the sky. She dismissed it as a shooting star, until she realized it was going the wrong direction.

She hurried into the house, to check on Dean, but he seemed

to be sleeping peacefully. She still could not understand what she had seen, but she settled down on the day couch, and soon dropped off to sleep. When morning came, she got up to check on him, but he was gone.

She remembered that thin light going up into the sky and told the doctor about it when he came to pronounce Dean dead. The doctor said Dean had died about 1:00 AM. He also said he wouldn't be surprised if the bright light Joy saw shooting skyward was Dean's soul departing this earth.

35

A Mother's Return

A doctor friend told me a story about when he lost his wife. She was only in her mid-fifties when she starting having heart problems. It was too soon for her to die, he said. After all, she still had her whole life ahead of her.

She soon found out that there was no way she could get help because what she had was such a progressive disease.

She was in the hospital by then, and time was getting short. Her husband was sitting by her bed. She started to smile, and then she told her husband not to worry, she was going to heaven, and her mother was coming for her.

The doctor told me that he could feel, but could not see, a presence around them. He knew someone was there that was not of this world. He saw his wife's hand lift up and knew her mother had probably come to get her, as she seemed so at peace.

You Live Forever, You Live Forever... / Gladys Hargis

36

Her Faith Never Wavers

I had a friend with a young daughter who had never been sick except for colds and the general diseases of childhood. A happy child, and so full of life, she was looking forward to her sixteenth birthday.

She had a secret that she did not want to share with her mother: she had been having sharp pains in her side.

After suffering for a couple of weeks, she gave up and told her mom who immediately called their family doctor. He asked them to come in and he would run tests.

The news was bad and it was, as he suspected. The girl had waited too long. Cancer had gotten a head start, and nothing could be done to stop it.

The daughter took the news quite well. She told her mother that she had been feeling Angels around her and knew they had been watching over her for some time. She seemed to accept the fact that she would be going home to Heaven.

Her mother was greatly relieved, knowing that, with her teachings and reading the Bible to her daughter , she was prepared her for this journey.

The doctor told them both that they had time to travel, if they wanted to. He was certain the girl would go peacefully in her sleep, no matter where she was. And so they set off on a cruise.

They went to Italy, and France, and visited the Alps. After about thirty days of wandering around Europe, the daughter died peacefully in her sleep.

The mother told me that she had buried her daughter in a

grave in Switzerland, where she had wanted to be buried. She told me that she was so happy for the time she had her daughter, that she was a gift from God, and that God had only loaned the child to her for a little while.

What a wonderful faith they both had, to realize that we are all loaned out, and that God is truly our Father, who art in Heaven.

37

Praises

I have given this book to many of my friends who have thanked me for sharing it with them. Some have lost loved ones. I have been told that the message of God's eternal love brings them peace, comfort, and hope.

Let me tell you, my dear friend, there will be an Angel with you as you leave this world. If you love everyone as yourself, the Heavens will open up and receive you. But be aware: if you are evil, with evil thoughts, you will never see the light or the cleansing white cloud that washes away the old and makes you pure enough to see the Lord Most High.

I have only seen a speck of what is to come for all of us. But this I know: there is so much more to look forward to.

I feel blessed to have been able to get a hint of what the gates of Heaven have in store for us. It is truly wonderful and exciting, and it brings me peace.

And you and I *will* live forever.

You Live Forever, You Live Forever... / Gladys Hargis

PSALMS 73:23-25 KJV

Nevertheless I am continually with thee:
You will hold my right hand.
You will guide me with your counsel,
and afterward you will receive me into
glory.

Who do I have in heaven but you dear God.
And there is nothing here on earth but you that I desire.
My body and my heart might fail, but God is the strength of
my heart and my portion forever.

You Live Forever, You Live Forever… / Gladys Hargis

SCRIPTURES

I will say of the Lord, He is my refuge and my fortress: My God; in Him will I trust. *Psalm 91:2, KJV*

Let not your heart be troubled: ye believe in God, believe also in me. *John 14:1 KJV*

In my Father's house are many mansions: if it were not so, I would have told you. I go to prepare a place for you. And if I go and prepare a place for you, I will come again and receive you unto myself; that where I am, there ye may be also. *John 14:2-3, KJV*

115

You Live Forever, You Live Forever... / Gladys Hargis

The Heavens

I have a place to wander, beyond the space of time,
with Jesus as my Leader, to meet old friends of mine.

Where light never fails to be there, and my eyes can see so
bright,
the beauty of the heavenly realm is caught up in my sight.

There is a place for all of us to live eternally, to work, to play,
to visit, and to worship ... every day.

Our Leader is forever, not on the shelf of time.
He has laid a plan for us, so we can be sublime.

We will see our parents every day, to join them at the throne,
to worship our Great Leader, who will guide us in our home.

We have dropped our chains of earthly bonds, and feel free
from toil and strife.
Our loved ones will be there as well to enhance our life.

Heaven is a peaceful place to rest from earthly chores,
a place to be so happy, with God and His Angels galore.

A place where time will never end , as promised by the Lord .
I am glad to be a part of this, and happy to be on board.

Written by Gladys L. Hargis & her Angel
Nov. 28, 2010

You Live Forever, You Live Forever... / Gladys Hargis

AUTHOR'S NOTE

July 2015. I was laying down, taking a nap, when the telephone rang. The woman on the other end of the line said she was Esther Luttrell, an author herself, and asked if I was the Gladys Hargis who had written the book *You Live Forever*. I said yes. She told me that she had just read it and was touched. Then she hesitated.

I waited.

"May I ask who published it?" she finally asked.

I told her the name of the publisher. Without getting into a great many details, the bottom line is that she pointed out the number of technical errors in the book and asked if we could get together to talk about them. I was uncertain what she was getting at, but we arranged for her to come by my house the next day.

She arrived at the appointed hour and I was telling her how I came to write the book. As I explained my experience in Heaven, and the many things my husband and I had shared regarding that miracle, I commented on Warren's passing. That's when she glanced over my shoulder, to a photo on a shelf.

"Is that your second husband?" she asked.

I wondered where she got such a notion; I'd only had one husband. All I could think to say was the truth. "I've only had one husband."

Esther's mouth sort of fell open. She frowned and then she said, "When did he die?"

I told her that Warren had passed away November 24, 2012.

She seemed surprised, even perplexed. "Do you know how I came to have a copy of your book?" she asked.

I told her that I did not.

119

"Remember when you participated in an author event last winter at the local library?"

I remembered it very well. It was last December. The year was 2014. Two years after Warren's death.

Esther seemed unsure how to go on, but she made an effort. "I had a table there, too. I was packing up to leave when a pleasant-looking gentleman came up to me and said something to the effect that his wife would like me to have a copy of her book.

"I thought, oh dear... another book. Authors give each other books at these events, and I had a stack that I knew I'd never be able to read, as it was.

"The gentleman was so nice and I remember thinking that he was probably a minister or a missionary. He had that tranquil look in his eyes that you see in people who have a close relationship with God. I also noticed that, while most of us were dressed nicely, we were all very casual. This man, slight of stature with thinning brown hair, wore a very nice suit and a tie. He was saying, 'She died and spent two hours in heaven. She isn't really a writer, but she tells about her experience in her own words. Our minister read it and gave an entire sermon on it.' I confess he now had my attention. He went on, 'Other ministers, in other states, have read it and they've given sermons on it, too'.

"I looked at the book and noticed what a pretty cover it had. When I promised to read it, he said, 'She has a table in the rotunda. If you get a chance, come by and meet her.' I said I would. He smiled and walked away.

"When I finished gathering up my books, I helped another woman load up a push cart and took it to the parking lot for her. As I went through the rotunda, I noticed that everyone was gone. There was no one in that area.

"I have an eye condition," Esther explained, "that had kept me from being able to read print for about the last year and a half, so I wasn't able to keep my promise to the sweet man. One

120

day, several months later—the day I called you—I noticed that my vision seemed unusually sharp. I even asked myself if I could actually pick up a book and read it.

"I was sitting in the living room, on my sofa, and I looked around for something I might use to test my eyes. That's when I noticed your book lying beside my telephone. I wondered what it was doing there, that isn't where I keep books. In any case, I picked it up and read it all the way through, the first time I'd actually read a book in nearly two years.

"I was impressed and touched by its message, but it troubled me that it was in need of an editor. There were many technical errors. So, I looked you up in the phone book and here I am."

Esther shook her head in irony. "Your husband handed me this book." She opened it to the title page. "Look. It even says, 'To Esther, God bless, Gladys Hargis'."

I looked at the page and it was, indeed, my handwriting, though I had never met the woman until this moment.

My family was helping me with my books in the rotunda that day at the library, but they had not seen Warren or they would have told me, yet it turned out that others *had* seen him, too, though this was the first I'd heard of it.

Esther and I agree that Warren wanted the book to reach as many people as possible. He was asking her to give me a hand with editing the book—which she did.

All through my time in this world, I have had many miracles happened to me, but this one stands out as the one I hold near and dear to my heart.

To know that loved ones who are gone from this world are still around us is wonderful. To fully understand that only their body is gone, but their soul is here with us, is a blessing.

This is the gift that God has given us to remember and to be thankful for. He is the keeper of our soul and, one day, we *will* rejoin our loved ones in Heaven because we do live forever.

You Live Forever, You Live Forever... / Gladys Hargis

ABOUT THE AUTHOR

GLADYS HARGIS

Warren and I were married in Holton Kansas, July 31, 1949.
I graduated from Hoyt, High School, Hoyt, Kansas and continued
my education in Business College. I was employed by the Santa
Fe Railroad , while Warren joined the Topeka Fire Department.

I continued working until our son William was five months
old. Then we took in day care children, finally foster children.
We drove school buses part-time to help with our budget, so
we could continue to help support all the children we had taken
in to raise. In addition to William, I have three foster children,
Joanie, Sandra, and Donnie; eight foster grandchildren, and four
great grandchildren.

After Warren and I became empty nesters, we continued
working for the State of Kansas, Warren as a fire officer and I
worked as a driver for the mentally ill.

We eventually retired and moved to Topeka, Kansas, where
I make my home with our cats, Ollie and Bandit.

You Live Forever, You Live Forever... / Gladys Hargis

Notes

Notes:

_____

_____

_____

_____

_____

_____

_____

_____

_____

_____

_____

_____

_____

_____

_____

_____

_____

_____

Notes:

_____

_____

_____

_____

_____

_____

_____

_____

_____

_____

_____

_____

_____

_____

_____

_____

_____

_____

_____

You Live Forever, You Live Forever... / Gladys Hargis

BOOKS BY GLADYS HARGIS

YOU LIVE FOREVER, YOU LIVE FOREVER, YOU LIVE FOREVER

THE LAND BEYOND THE VEIL

Gladys Hargis books are available on Amazon in print, or may be ordered through any bookstore. They are also available as an eBook and may be purchased through Amazon/Kindle.

The author is always glad to hear from readers. Feel free to send her an email at ollieblack7@live.com.

You Live Forever, You Live Forever... / Gladys Hargis

Made in the USA
San Bernardino, CA
07 February 2017